HENRY

A Carriage Driving
Pony's Life And Adventures

AuthorHouse™ UK Ltd.
1663 Liberty Drive
Bloomington, IN 47403 USA
www.authorhouse.co.uk
Phone: 0800.197.4150

Published by AuthorHouse 09/18/2014

ISBN: 978-1-4969-9075-4 (sc)
ISBN: 978-1-4969-9076-1 (e)

authorHOUSE®

Introduction

This is basically a history of a carriage driving pony and it's owners over a period of some 2 years, although it is not quite as clear cut as that.

It is a true story, taken from our memories and records, and looked at from all sides.

Henry's comments are as we thought they would be from his perspective.

Over time, the three of us shed blood, sweat and tears, so our relationship and bond became incredibly strong.

Even when suffering from a most painful and debilitating condition called laminitis, Henry always pushed on and forwards with true grit, never giving up.

We for our part never gave up on him, pushing him on when fit and well, and we had some incredible drives together.

In the darkest moments of this crippling, cruel condition we nursed him back to health, sometimes with tears in our eyes.

So sit back, read on, and share our journey.

We meet for the first time

Chapter One...

In the beginning an ambition

Eddie:

I guess it all started some years ago when my wife Lorna and I regularly fished lakes in West Sussex. Access to these lakes was through beautifully maintained paddocks and fields. At the entrance was a large metal sign with Carriage Driving Centre, and an embossed print of what looked like a horse with wheels attached to its rear! It made me comment to Lorna that 'Carriage driving must be a lovely way to get around'. However, that was the end of that particular ambition for a long time.

This was probably because neither of us knew one end of a horse from the other! That is apart from the certain knowledge, that one end bit, and the other kicked!

To be honest, at that time and for some time to come, learning to carriage drive or anything to do with horses, took a very low priority in our busy lives.

After several years we changed employment and location from West Sussex to Buckinghamshire. Our new employment was as housekeeper and gardener, to a retired couple, their house and acres of land.

Included in our new employment was a lovely detached cottage, just set back from a minor road, and beautiful woodlands. Now, both approaching sixty and semi retired, we had plenty of spare time on our hands, but for me fishing no longer had the appeal of the past.

One summer morning, whilst digging in the garden, I heard the clatter of hooves, somehow different from the noise of a ridden horse, and was delighted to see a shetland pony pulling an exercise cart complete with lady driver!

To cut a long story short, I soon made friends with her and over the course of six months, in exchange for simple horsey tasks, she helped me to achieve my ambition of carriage driving around the pretty lanes.

The pony was so well schooled and behaved that I rather think it was driving me!

My ambition was finally realised when I was trusted to go out for short drives with Lorna. Then just as I thought all was going very well the pony was sold, so that was the end of that! Having put in a lot of hours and hard work to learn the basics of carriage driving, I was left in a bit of a muddle. I am a slow learner, so should I just give up, or go down the long road of purchasing a horse and equipment, and all of the huge expenses that would entail.

After much discussion Lorna and I decided to go for the latter option. I had only limited experience, and that was with a shetland pony, so I had a bit of a 'bee in my bonnet' that a shetland pony was the animal for us.

However, after speaking to a couple of horsey people, the general concensus was to go for at least a medium size pony, one that would be able to cope with the inclines and hills we are surrounded by.

So 'biting the bullet' we started to scour the internet in our search for a pony. For some reason, only known to me, I was sure that what I wanted was a white mare, age immaterial, but no more than 11hh.

This 'wonder horse' would be bombproof in traffic, well behaved, fully trained, experienced and suitable for a pair of complete novices!

Didn't want much did we!

Chapter Two...

The search for the wonder horse

Eddie:

The selection of horses and ponies was staggering, as was the choice of equipment, carriages, tack, bits and so on. Our first visit was to look at a 11hh pony.

Described as a perfect gentleman (not my prefered mare!) trained to ride (pretty irrelevant as neither Lorna or myself had sat on a horse before!) and trained to drive(this was the bit that we desired!)

The young lady owner greeted us warmly and introduced us to a rather scruffy looking pony, and an even more scruffy exercise cart and harness!

To be blunt Lorna and I were soon side by side on an exercise cart with, what I considered to be, a huge horse at the end of a set of reins!

After a frightening 20 minutes 'drive', along a main road, then around bumpy commonland, we arrived back at the pony's stable, disturbingly shaken, stirred and with almost white hair!

Not his fault, but certainly not for us So..back to the drawing board.

It took us a few days to recover and summon enough courage to continue our search for our lifetime companion.

Lorna:

After avidly and enthusiastically searching an internet site a rather good looking pony stopped me dead in my tracks.

As I looked in detail at the picture and information I thought, wrong colour (chestnut... Eddie hates chestnut!) 13hh(too big..Eddie wants something tiny!) Too expensive..(we had a tight budget!)but it says bombproof, well schooled, excellent manners, suitable for beginners.

He does look nice though..Hmmmmm.

Eddie:

When Lorna showed me the picture I took an instant dislike to this pony who was called Henry. I had only driven a little shetland and to be honest this pony looked huge!

However, it was only an hour away, so an arrangement was made for a viewing. The owners sounded nice enough on the phone and almost promised us the moon.

Henry:

I knew something was up and so I was highly suspicious! I had been groomed until my coat shone and told to be on my very, very best behaviour. I was now nine years old and had spent most of that time stuck in various fields with other horses. I never knew my horsey father, and my mother, a lovely pony whose breath smelt of sweet hay, left me when I was very young. I was now with my third owners. My first two owners were never cruel but one day, when I was quite young, a human who was much too heavy sat on my back and hurt me. So I never allowed anyone to sit on me again.

Oh.. all my owners had tried and tried to do 'riding' training with me...but I wasn't having any of it! It just hurt so much.

After many boring years, eating my way through fields and doing nothing, I became ill in my feet. They really hurt when I moved around, so I often had to stay in my room for weeks on end. I was very unhappy.

My third and current owners didn't try to sit on my back but put wheels on me and

I dragged them along a bit. It felt different to having someone on my back and they called it 'driving' training. To be honest it didn't hurt my back at all but the metal bit in my mouth hurt, the various straps on my body didn't fit too well, and I didn't like the wheels much! I hadn't been doing it very long, but at least I was now going out to new places, and stretching my legs. Anyway that's my story so far.

Eddie:

We met the owners of Henry who seemed honest, pleasant and reasonable enough, but there was a tiny alarm bell ringing at the back of my mind, which I put down to nervousness on my part.

A lovely looking chestnut pony was shown to us. He was in good condition, well looked after and relaxed. He was though, a gelding, bigger, and a different colour to what I wanted.

BUT...when eye contact was made, something definitely clicked. It is difficult to explain but kindness, intelligence and trust oozed out of this pony. I was completely hooked and I wanted him!

A short drive with the owners instantly made me aware he was not perfect...that little alarm bell was tinkling, but I was besotted!

Lorna:

As soon as Henry came up to us I knew he was for us. There was something about him that seemed to beg us to take him.

My only worry was that Eddie might not agree, he was so adamant about the colour and size of pony he had set his mind on. Thankfully my fears were unfounded.

Henry:

As soon as I saw these two humans I knew they were for me. First chance, last chance, I wanted them. Caring, warm, kind and a way with animals. I felt very, very comfortable with them. After a walk they groomed me and I was on my best behaviour.

I kept flashing my eyes at the woman and walking around her with my best steps. As soon as I nuzzled her I knew I was in with a chance.

They put my wheels on for a little drive. I was very nervous, but I just walked, trying to ignore the monsters in the hedge, so they wouldn't see what a coward I really was.

A final grooming and off they went. Soon I would know. I wanted them so much that I couldn't settle or sleep that night.

Eddie:

After a long talk with Lorna we decided to purchase Henry. With fingers crossed we arranged for a vet to give Henry a medical. We found out that he had a cataract in one eye and, very probably, a condition called laminitis in the past.

We knew that all three of us had a long hard road ahead of us. But, ever ready as complete novices are, we thought we were prepared. Little did we know how long and hard the road to success would be.

Lorna:

It was a long time since I had been so excited about a new arrival, and now, our very own and first equinine, was being delivered within days!

Although I knew Eddie had little experience I had faith in his ability as a carriage driver(whip).I was looking forward to my new role as the backstep (groom)and helping to ensure our pony was a happy, safe driving animal.

Little did I know I was in for a sharp and sudden shock.

Chapter Three...

Henry comes home

Henry:

I walked into the room on wheels with some apprehension. This was going to be either very bad or very good news.

After a long, noisy, bumpy journey the doors opened and 'joy of joys' the two humans were there and they were smiling! I couldn't help myself and gave a big 'Ninny'. I now felt that I really had a life in front of me with these new owners as a mum and dad.

They led me into a new field where I met my horsey neighbours. That first night I was kicked, bitten, chased and bullied by the other two bigger horses. However, being new and much smaller, I was expecting this, and as the field was very big, I managed to mostly keep out of the way!

Eddie:

The horsebox arrived and, after a bit of encouragement, Henry stepped off. The lead rope was on and we now had our pony to do as we wished. Money and horse passport changed hands...the deal was done!

Lorna:

We both got up early to see Henry after his first night and, horror of horrors, he was nowhere to be seen! Panic set in. Then we spotted our pony, hidden away by some nettles, right at the other end of the huge field.

We walked up to him and he warmly greeted us. Over the next couple of days we tried to bond with him by grooming him and walking him down the lane and in the woods.

This was a lovely time and it seemed the three of us enjoyed each others' company. Then on the third day, when we called him, he came galloping to meet us .A very happy moment!

Eddie:

All went well for a couple of days, we could even walk him the short distance to our cottage, and tie him up on a wall ring outside .There we could feed, groom and pet him easily. Until that is, he spotted another horse being ridden in the woods, on the other side of the road.

His ears went back, his eyes went wild and he snorted! He was absolutely petrified. It was almost impossible to control him and he took no heed of my attempts to calm him.

I realised then that we had a problem. This was not the bombproof, well schooled pony we had been promised.

The next day he continued to be nervous and he spooked at any kind of traffic. Cars, cyclists, branches, birds, paper, leaves. You name it, he spooked at it!

I decided there and then that he was too much for us and as we had a verbal agreement with the previous owners, that they would have him back if we had any problems, phoned them to come and collect him.

However, they went back on their word, refusing to take him back. I was absolutely gutted, feeling furious and disappointed with myself for trusting them in the first place. I really should have known better and listened to that alarm bell!

Lorna:

When Eddie told me of his decision I sat on the stairs and cried. Although I knew that it was all going wrong, I felt we were letting Henry down, and not really giving him a chance.

But Eddie was right he was too much for us. It was obvious we were too green, so was he, a bad combination. However, when the previous owners refused to have him back it made me feel even more determined to keep him , somehow train him, no matter what it took.

Henry:

Stupid, stupid, stupid. I'd messed up and could tell the two humans were not so happy with me now. I'd only been with them a few days and they were very unhappy about something. Probably my lack of courage and manners, but there were monsters everywhere , there really were. I tried to tell them but they didn't listen. Now I was really worried that I was off to another home yet again.

Eddie:

After much talking and heart searching discussion between us, Lorna and I decided we would have no further communication with the people who sold us Henry.

We were stuck with a pony who needed retraining or, much worse, training! We had no money left to pay a professional trainer, or know any carriage driving friends who could help us with our predicament. We were, stupidly, complete novices...all three of us.

Lorna:

I have never given up on anything in my life and knew that our only course of action was to go back to basics. Train or retrain Henry to what we wanted for ourselves, a happy, confident and safe driving pony.

No matter how long, or how much frustration and sheer hard work it took, we could and would do it. This would be our project. I felt Henry had already had enough let downs in his life and he deserved better than that.

We would read all the books and magazines, watch dvds, ask questions and take some lessons for ourselves in basic horsemanship and rein handling.

Eddie would be the driver/whip, main trainer and master. I would be the groom/ backstep, harness person and safe place. And so it began.

Henry:

Thankfully things started to change for the better. For the next couple of weeks I was walked, groomed, talked to and fussed over. I even went out with the wheels on for some short trips. Although I was still very terrified of anything and everything.

None of my equipment fitted and the wheels were terribly uncomfortable. Mum and Dad had lots of patience, but I could feel they were getting frustrated.

I tried so hard to do what they wanted even though the metal bar in my mouth and the straps round my head hurt. And yes.. there were monsters on the road, hiding in the hedges, lurking in the woods, so I was scared.

I tried, but I just couldn't get them to understand, that I really was not the bravest pony in the world. I really needed them to understand that I was trying my hardest. Then I had a fantastic idea which would change everything.

That night, my spirit left my body..and I went on a little visit.

Eddie:

Both Lorna and I were getting angry and disappointed with ourselves and frustrated at Henry's lack of ability and confidence. Even the slightest object would make him spook or shy..sometimes worse!

I really was at the end of my tether, and although Henry was a lovely pony, he was a huge investment in both our time and money and we were getting little in return.

We knew that some of the other owners at the stables were, in all honesty, laughing at our lack of progress. But they could give little advice, as they didn't have any driving experience themselves.

Lorna, as always, took it all in her stride. As for me, I was getting so uptight that I was loosing sleep, my temper and my enthusiasum. Then one night it all changed and everthing became clear.

I remember being completely exhausted by our lack of progress and, after a couple of stiff drinks, went to bed and managed to fall asleep and dream.

In my dream world Henry came to me glowing with sadness and love. He then simply said 'I'm just scared Dad'. I was awake in seconds and can still feel the realisation that I suddenly knew the way forwards!

Henry was just a big, lovely coward. Obviously, the equipment we were using, and the way we training him, wasn't making him feel comfortable or safe. So we would have to do everthing we could to get his confidence and trust in us.

It was as if a light, a very bright light, had gone on in my head. It was as if a huge weight had been lifted from my shoulders. Now there would only be going forwards. No more moaning or groaning and feeling sorry for ourselves. Lorna got a huge unexpected hug!

Lorna:

After a restless nights sleep Eddie told me about his dream. Overnight he seemed to be an almost different person, more confident and enthusiastic. It was like he had come out of the dark and into the light, his head had found a way forward!

We decided to get rid of all the current old driving equipment. I then spent hours measuring Henry and looking at new carriages and harness on the internet. This time not for us or Henry secondhand!

More money was removed from our savings and a pony size exercise cart, complete with disc brakes, swingletree and pneumatic tyres was ordered. A lightweight, but very strong, durable and adjustable harness, that would fit like a glove, was also ordered and, after careful measurement of Henry's mouth, a Liverpool driving bit.

Soon more necessary purchases were added to the list of must haves! ie Driving whip, long reining roller and lungeing equipment. Information books and DVDs on the theory and practice of carriage driving soon adorned our coffee table, ready for referencing on many occasions.

We even changed Henry's diet to a good vitamin packed feed, with magnesium and calmer supplements, that he would look forward to after his work was done. Lessons for us on basic horsemanship, rein handling, harnessing and driving were booked with Chris, a local LHHI (Light Horse Handling Instructor).Chris was very sympathetic to our needs and gave us, no frills, good solid advice and tuition.

Now at last we felt we were in with a chance! Happy days! So fully armed with polos and carrots...it all started.

Henry in new Harness

Chapter Four...

A bag of carrots and a pocket full of polos.

Henry:

Dad(my new master) and mum(my safe place) continued to take me for walks. I rather hoped the measuring up with bits of string was a sign of better and exciting, but safe times, to come. I definitely liked my new food and had a delicious bowl for breakfast and supper with lots of fruit..Yum yum!

I was slowly realising that I had to work for a bit of carrot or a polo mint...no work... no treat. I remember, one day in particular, when dad tried to get me to do something that I was never able to fully understand before.

This was to simply stand, and not move, no matter what demons or temptations were around. He made it quite clear to me (and I'm not stupid)that our days would start, continue and finish with a mint only when I obeyed and stood still until told to move.

It took a few days but bit by bit(excuse the pun!)I understood and did what he wanted. To say dad was beside himself is an understatement, and both he and I were shell shocked at our sudden progress.

Eddie:

The most important part of a carriage horse's training is to stand on request, at any time, in any place or situation. It is the fundamental building block of training that is essential to safety in the carriage.

However, yes you've guessed it..Henry couldn't and wouldn't stand still for more than a second or two. He either moved forwards, backwards or in circles and sometimes, playfully, reared up! Says a lot for his past trainers!

For a month I would go to his field, sometimes six times a day, trying to get him to respond to the command 'stand'. Lorna came with me on occasions to observe the training and any progress made. More often than not she would leave early, shaking her head in despair, as Henry walked in circles around me.

But late one evening, it suddenly happened...Henry stood still on command! I nearly fainted with relief...or shock! After a further couple of days I could completely walk around Henry as he stood like a statue. I waved sticks and whips at him and he stood still until given the command to move.

After a further couple of days I could stand behind him and give him the command to 'walk on'. We would then continue to walk across his field, pony in front, master behind. At last Henry was walking on and standing at my command! We celebrated.. Henry ate a lot of polo mints that week ..and I drank a lot of beer!

Lorna:

Eddie would often sneak up to Henry's field to 'poo' pick, bond with Henry, and make an attempt at training.. ie try to get Henry to respond to commands! Mostly without success! Many a time I would watch them with pity as they both struggled along.

In fact,I remember saying to Eddie, that he would never get Henry to stand for any length of time, and I was quite despondent about what we were going to do in the future. But no trainer could ever have had as much patience and perseverance as Eddie, he was determined, and I was very proud of them both!

One lunchtime(we often had our sandwich lunch with Henry)Eddie asked me to watch for a while as he talked to Henry. My sandwich nearly fell out of my hands when I saw Henry respond to every command Eddie gave him.

He walked, halted and stood. I was amazed..they were both now working in perfect unison together. No headcollar, no rope, no reins..just verbal commands. Fantastic day!

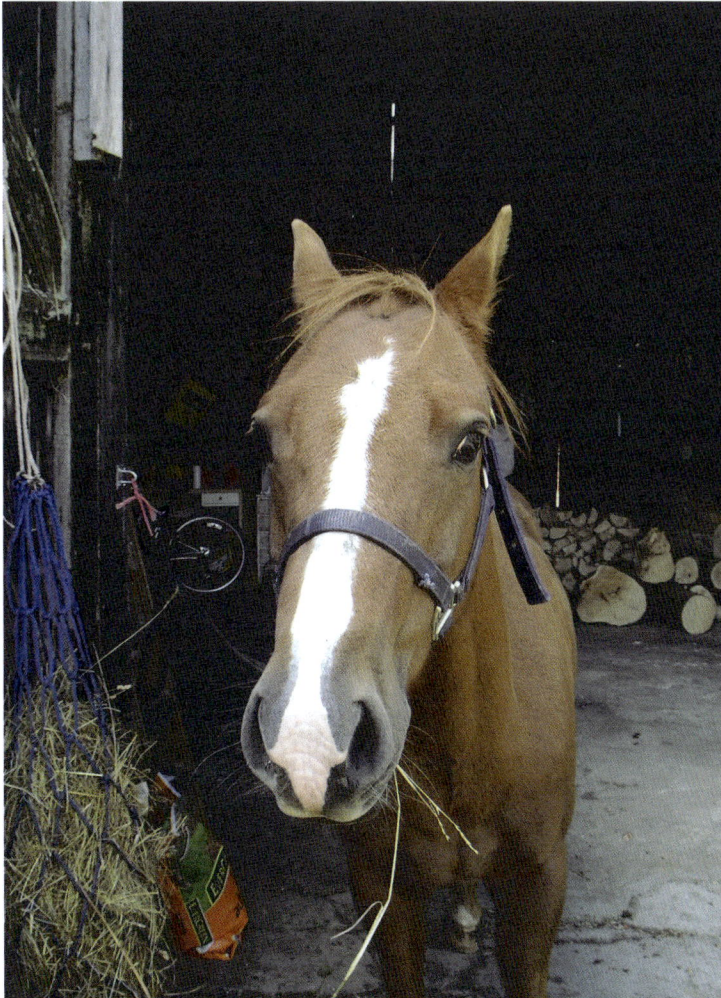

Henry trying hard to stand still

Henry and Eddie

18

Chapter Five...

Let the real training commence!

Eddie:

Unfortuanetly we didn't have the luxury of an enclosed training arena for proper schooling purposes. At first we tried some lessons in a field, but all Henry wanted to do was eat the grass and look around, frequently loosing his concentration! Although he would be spending his working life on the highway we didn't think it fair on any of us, or the general public, to do all his training there. We needed to find a suitable enclosed training area where we could teach the basics in safety. Then, it suddenly dawned on us, we had a reasonably suitable training area on our doorstep! It was, infact, the gravel courtyard between our cottage and the main house. It was a very small and imperfect rectangle approx 40 yds x 20 yds, set on a slight slope! Around all the edges were bushes, shrubs, outbuildings and walls. At it's entrance was a cattle grid, so to get into the courtyard from the road, Henry had to negotiate and squeeze through a small side gate. He only just fitted! At the vision of this manoeuvre, some people will laugh or shake their heads in disbelief, but this was all we had. We could only use this area when nobody else or any parked cars were around. We also had to leave the area in an immaculate condition after use, crazily raking the gravel back into place!

However, in this tiny space, we practised 'lungeing, 'harnessing up' and 'putting to'. We even drove Henry round and round in the exercise cart making him stop, stand, walk and trot! Also, while I walked Henry around with his bridle and blinkers on, Lorna would walk around with wheelbarrows, cycles, mowers, ladders, strimmers and banging buckets! You name it we did it. Anything to get him confident! I remember once Lorna even drove the car slowly behind him, tooting the horn! Henry eventually took it all in his stride, and sometimes even seemed a little bored with it all! Although the area was small, if we hadn't used it, we would never have achieved all that we did. I guess the advice from us is to make the most of what you've got, and if not close to home then at home! Like us you will be surprised at what you can utilise in the training process. I can remember our satisfaction when eventually Henry stood still, and didn't move, while we dragged a rather untidy scarecrow decorated with balloons around him. He looked at us with a total disbelief at our antics! That reminds me...training can be such fun!!

Henry and Lorna in the courtyard

Chapter Six...

Bazil's story

I'd been mum and dad's spoilt little doggie for a long time now. Always loved, pampered, played with, walked, fed..truly cossetted. However, I have a put up with a lot over time, as they welcomed into our family, budgies, quails, bantams, rabbits, fish and a pigeon.. who is still here!

I've been pecked, bitten, kicked and hissed at, but have always taken it all in my stride and been happy, contented and grateful. There is one thing though that I have always wanted to share my home with, and which I dream about at night, that is a pussycat with a big, preferably ginger, fluffy tail.

We could play doggie games all day, and in the evening we could snuggle up together, and the pussycat's big tail would cover me and keep me warm, whilst we drift off to sleep. Oh joy! However, nothing has happened on the cat front yet...apart from of course the incident at the village annual animal blessing.

That was when my dream ginger pussycat appeared, held in the arms of a lady. I remember the long fluffy, ginger tail swishing just above me..tempting me to play..or so I thought. To cut a long story short, the lady ran off wailing, as did the pussycat. Somehow I managed to end up with a load of ginger fluff in my mouth! Not a good day. That was the end of that, or so I thought.

I remember feeling very suspicious, but excited, when I listened to mum and dad talking one morning. Something about a big ginger with a lovely tail. Dad was putting huge wads of paper into his back pocket (Something they call money!)Was this my surprise at long last?.. it certainly was!

Later, when I was snuggled up happily in the back of my mobile bedroom (car),I heard the main gate to our cottage creak open. This was it, my dream had come true, I spotted a flash of ginger out of the corner of my eye. Then horror of horrors, they led in a huge panting, salivating monster! This was no pussycat!

This was the beast from hell! It was a very, very big horse dribbling bits of dead dog from its teeth. I froze in fear as it fixed me with the eyes of a devil and stood very close to me. Mum and dad broke my paralysis by saying 'Baz this is Henry the new member of our family'.

I didn't know whether to laugh or cry. This really was taking the mickey out of me. The monster dropped its head, fixed me with an evil grin and sniffed. Probably to see if I would make a tasty treat!

Dad assured me all was okay and that I would soon come to love this Horse called Henry (of all things).I really could have leapt at dad, then and there, and bit him where it hurt!

However, overtime, things did get better. We had a grudging respect for each other and, I admit, he did look out for and protect me. He was like a big brother, he had a wicked sense of humour ! Soon I was able to get into his room, which was full or lovely warm straw, and hide my sticks.

I could run between his legs, have a look in his oversize food bowl, and he never once tried to kick me. Not so for the other dogs at the stables..Frankie, Tico, Roxy all tried to get into the room to get at my sticks.

Henry's ears would go back with his head forwards, like a striking snake, and the other dogs would shoot out of Henry's room, tails between their legs..never to return!

I've been on plenty of long walks with Henry in the woods. I've even been out on the wheels a few times..he says he finds that scary..well so do I...but mum and dad reassure us both with their love and trust. Now every year, I arrive at the animal blessing in style, on Henry's carriage. I have to say he is a very, very special friend.

The downside to our friendship is having to get up early every morning with dad when it is still dark, as I love my nice warm bed. But in rain, snow, wind, frost we have to walk up a big hill to see Henry, clean up his 'poo' and feed him.

Still, musn't complain...as I am a very fit doggie, with no surplus fat. Thanks Henry!

Henry driving Bazil to the animal blessing

Henry in his stable

Chapter Seven...

Escape to the Horse Hotel

Henry:

I was fairly happy with my room and field when my owners first had me. Ok..so the room was dark, cold and damp, but dad tried to make it cosy for me. The field was huge and very nice, mum and dad visited me lots of times everyday, because it was so close to their house.

I only had one horsey friend, same size and colour as me..called Toto. He had a medical condition called 'Cushings syndrome', and like me, was not mean't to eat too much grass, especially if it was of the tasty kind!

One night, when all was quiet and dark we decided to have a bit of an adventure! A bit of escapology! Toto pushed the field gate with his head and I pushed it with my rear...and joy of joys, after much pushing it opened.

We slunk out quietly, like two thieves in the night, savouring happily our freedom! A graze here and a graze there, sweet grass, wonderful! Eventually we found a very nice garden, full of goodies, so we really, really stuffed ourselves. The owner must have told on us because bright and early the next day dad came to catch me.

I knew he was in a very bad mood because he scowled at me and muttered dark things. He took me back to my field and I felt very ashamed. Dad stomped off, still in a mood, and still muttering dark things!

The next day mum and dad came to take me out for a drive. There were a lot of buckets, feed bags and hay packed onto my wheels, then off we went, with my extra burden. I couldn't work it out but knew they were both still upset with me.

Up the hill we went, but this time turned left, and walked down a tiny lane I had never been down before. My ears pricked up and I trotted a bit..I could smell horses..nice horses! We stopped at a gate that opened and closed by itself. It was a bit alarming, I had never seen a gate that opened and closed by itself before!

We drove into a beautiful, clean yard. Mum and dad got off, which they do at the end of a drive, I was confused, where was I and why? They both came to my head and smiled huge smiles. Then they said something like 'welcome to your new home'. I looked around and saw lots of clean and tidy rooms.

Each room had an interested horse looking at me over the door. Only one room was empty, the room that caught the sun most, and on the door was my name..Henry. I stomped, I neighed, I ninnnied and even with the metal bar still in my mouth I gave mum and dad a kiss. They got the wheels and everything off me and led me into my room.

Light, dry, sunny and warm with a haynet, water tub, treat ball, food bowl, it was all there. It was a huge room and, because of the way the room was made, I could see my neighbours on both sides. I could also put my head over the door and see all the other horses.

This must be a horse hotel, and I was staying! I saw dad talking to a lady and, as always, he put his hand in his back pocket and gave her a load of paper. But he was still smiling. This was it, I was home, safe, warm, happy and I had new friends.

Mum took me to my new field, it was fantastic. I was left to get to know some new friends Billy (a cob) and Lance a little (a shetland).Both were nice, and for once, I was the boss! I was in charge! A quick nip or kick and no-one got near mum and dad.

I've been in this luxury hotel ever since and enjoyed every single day. Maybe I will stay for the rest of my days, even when I can no longer pull the 'wheels' up the hill, or walk through the woods with mum, dad and my doggie mate Bazil.

April(Manager Horse Hotel):

Henry has been resident with us for just over a year, and a real credit to his owners, who are besotted with him. A very sweet natured, mischevious pony, full of character and full of himself! As he is the only driving pony in our stables he is always spoilt by the staff, who love his cheekiness and good manners.

However, it hasn't always been like that. I first met Eddie and Lorna as I was driving my car up to my stables, they were walking a rather boisterous chestnut pony on a lead rope towards the village. As a horsey person I smiled and waved in acknowledgment to them.

Over the coming weeks I saw them almost on a daily basis, struggling with this pony, trying to get it to walk and respond to commands. I must say, although they looked determined and were always smiling, they seemed to be having no success at all. The pony, who I later came to know as Henry, appeared to have a mind and will of his own!

Eddie and Lorna also nearly always appeared to have bits of debris attached to them, hedgerow, twigs, bits of fencing. In fact they sometimes looked like scarecrows. On my drives daily down the lane I started to notice bits of damaged hedgerow and fencing, I put two and two together, they were definetly having a hard time!

However, as time went on, Henry appeared to be much more controllable and obedient. His owners seemed more confident and the damage to the surrounding countryside became non-existent! I witnessed their progress as they changed from walking with a lead rope to long reining, then eventually, to harness and cart. At first it was with Eddie in the driving seat and Lorna walking in front, normally with a pouch of carrots! Finally after about six months of constant perseverance, I was absolutely delighted when, one afternoon, Henry went happily and confidently past my car. His two owners were sitting on the cart and gave me a wave with big smiles on their faces!

Overtime I've had lots of horsey chats with them, and the rest is history. We are now good friends, and as you know, Henry is happily resident at our stables. They both still ask questions and seek advice, and continue to exercise and enjoy Henry.A lovely result!

Henry by the pub fence

Chapter Eight....

Learning lessons

1. The travelling man...

Eddie:

Before purchasing Henry I had made friends with a member of the travelling community who had a past steeped in gypsy culture. I used to watch enviously, as he and some very young members of his family, effortlessly enjoyed the pastime of trotting around the lanes. After hearing of my troubles of woe with Henry,he offered to take me out on his sulky(gypsy high speed trotting cart).

We met at the village pub, and after a quick drink, I was seated side by side with my friend on a skeletal, uncomfortable cart, that had aluminium struts, webbing, and cycle wheels!

In front, pulling this traditional contraption, was an even more skeletal looking horse! So began my initiation in how to drive a cart with confidence. We trotted uphill, downhill, on the flat, over verges, over grass tracks, on lanes, through villages, past cars, bikes and tractors...the horse never blinked an eyelid no matter what was expected of it!

We drove through every village and hamlet for miles only stopping to refuel at every available pub. This was obviously for a quick drink, but also for some respite for the horse! I was not allowed to put my hand in my pocket to fund a single drink or pub sandwich.

I was given much horsey advice and sympathy without any arrogance or condescending attitude from my friend. Eventually I was dropped off at home, a bit worse for wear, and off he went for another five mile drive home assuring me he would be 'stopping off' for just one more!

I make no judgement on the way he worked his animal, and am truly amazed and astounded by his confidence,in himself and his horse. From that day on I drove with a new found confidence, pushing Henry on to what I knew we could achieve together, enjoying this pastime of carriage driving and companionship very much. My friend's ground breaking piece of advice was to drive Henry to the pub and tie him up to a fence that was next to the main road. He assured me that leaving Henry tied up like this, so he could stand and watch the passing traffic for an hour, would give him confidence. We did as he suggested many times, but stayed a very short distance away from him...just in case!

This experience really was the turning point in my driving with Henry. After this trip out with my friend I surprised myself, Lorna and Henry with my change of attitude..I was confident...I was in control...and we were going to enjoy ourselves and have fun! So I pushed Henry onwards and upwards to a previously unthought of driving experience and have never looked back.

So..thank you my friend, I may not agree with all of your advice and driving techniques. I probably will never emulate the way you drive horses.. BUT..you really changed my attitude and approach to this wonderful old, traditional pastime. So thank you!

Lorna:
When Eddie went past our cottage at a rate of knots, with a white face and wide grimace, I thought he would never want to be behind a driving a horse again! But he returned, safely, with more confidence and ambition to succeed than ever before.

Henry:
It is a very strange thing, but after dad went out training with his friend, he started using the words 'In the pub'. It means turning sharp left, lining up, and standing still by

the fence, watching all matters of good and bad things pass by, and getting a decent bit of orange or lemon 'titbit' from someone called a barman!

We don't go often but, as you can imagine, 'In the pub' has become one of my favourite sayings. We sometimes even take friends there, so I have really good manners and am on my best behaviour..Yummy fruit!

2. The Christmas Tree....

Eddie:

On a few of our trips out with Henry in December, we noted that many passing vehicles were carrying the traditional christmas tree home on their roof racks. We had to be extra vigilant when these hazards approached, try to keep Henry focused on the road ahead, and not this new and strangest of sights! Oneday, whilst out in the car, we saw that a christmas tree had been erected on the village green.

It was huge, and we had no doubt Henry wouldn't like it, magically and suddenly appearing on a well known, trouble free route. We decided on a cunning plan. We would walk Henry down to the village green and introduce him to the tree then, when we next drove by on the carriage, he would know it would be there and accept it as a normal sight.

So off we set, walking nonchalantly the half mile or so to the village. Henry was in a happy mood munching here and there on the journey, as if he was stopping at his favourite takeaways. We approached the village green and there was the tree, tall and waving in the slight breeze, aglow with seasonal brightness and lights! With a deep breath we approached closer...Henry stopped, looked, then bent his head to graze on the grass.

We let him spend a bit of time circling the tree and grazing at its roots. Then we continued our journey back home feeling very pleased with ourselves and our plan. We were very confident, that next time we drove down to the village, Henry would not see the tree as an alien monster! A few days later off we went for a drive to the village. Henry trotted confidently, knowing this route well by now, and hoping no doubt, to meet a friendly carrot bearing villager or vicar's wife.

Approaching the village ,we held our breath, crossed fingers, and continued to drive on the road past the green and tree! Then we did our usual turn, back around the green, for home. Henry suddenly stopped dead in his tracks, nearly catapulting me from the driving seat and Lorna over the rein rail. He froze, feet firmly planted on the road surface. He was not going to budge one inch! Lorna as usual quickly got to his head for control.

Then I spotted the cause of alarm..the electric cable, that was supplying energy to the tree lights, ran across the road in Henry's path..He had never seen this before!!!Lorna then had to jump on the cable, stroke it, dance on it, hop back and forwards over it, so that Henry knew it was safe to cross. This he did, at a fair speed and without so much as a backwards glance, so that Lorna had to run and jump up onto the backstep whilst pony and carriage were moving fast for home!

Lorna:
We thought we were so clever. But again a lesson was learnt. You can fool a horse some of the time, but he will always catch you out if you aren't clever enough. So again I had to show Henry, as I have done on many occasions, that all is okay. After all I am his safe place!

Henry:
Good thing I have a mum to get swallowed up first if there is a monster or, in this case, a deadly snake, waiting to gobble you up! Tree, what tree?

3. The Flapping Man

Eddie:
Henry was well into his training and we were having many safe and happy drives of up to seven miles at a time. He was now pretty much perfect with traffic and farm

vehicles. In the early days we had to desensitise him to cyclists, this was because of the sheer volume of cyclists on the road in our area, and because many of them were very unpredictable in their actions and road sense towards other traffic.

Henry was now confidently sharing his routes with any number of cyclists. Cyclists would approach from the front or from behind Henry and he was not concerned at all. So, as you can imagine, we felt really pleased. Until that is...Henry was trotting homewards, finishing a long and arduous drive, when I spotted an approaching cyclist in the distance. Like most cyclists he was wearing a florescent, yellow, jacket. No problems so far, but then he waved and undid his very baggy lightweight jacket. As he was travelling, at some speed towards us, the wind caught the jacket and blew it around him like the wings of some predatory bird! Well this , on reflection ,is how we thought Henry saw it! In a thrice Henry spooked, snorted and turned completely around, nearly tipping us out of the carriage. Next was a 20 yard bolt at high speed before I managed to stop a terrified Henry by steering him into the grass verge. Lorna, as usual, was off the carriage and at Henry's head to save us all!

It took some moments before she could calm him down. The poor cyclist passed us at a walking pace but soon speeded up when Henry turned to face him with ears back, a livid snort and very malevolent look. We got Henry home safely, however things were never the same and it took several months before Henry would accept cyclists again, but even then very, very suspiciously!

Lorna:

Again I learnt a lesson. Enjoy the drive but never let your guard down. Things can and do go wrong in an instant!

Henry:

This was a terrifying experience. One of the worst. I don't know what it was, but it was coming to kill me, and mum and dad. So, I had to turn and run for our lives. Very, very frightening! Never trust a cyclist again!

Henry at the village shop

Chapter Nine...

Stories to tell of Thrills and Spills

1. The horse in the woods...

Eddie:

It was only after a couple of days of owning Henry that we realised what a spooky, nervous pony he was. We were into our third day of making friends and bonding with him. He happily walked from his stables to our cottage so we decided to tie him up to our outside garden wall and give him a groom.

The lane is a very short distance, approx 10 yards from our cottage wall, a few cars had gone past with Henry ignoring them whist he enjoyed the grooming and subsequent titbits. However, in the woods on the other side of the lane, a horse and rider ambled along the bridleway.

Henry immediately went rigid, with ears back and eyes wide like saucers, his breathing turned into a huge snort. In a split second, terrified of this horse in the woods, he pulled back away from his wall tie. Although I managed to get hold of his lead rope quickly, I realised there was a problem, it was as if I didn't exist.

With another huge snort he pulled right back, taking with him the wall chain, twine, wall ring and nails complete with several bricks! He headed back in the direction of his stables complete with parts of the wall and me hanging on to his lead rope! Once free he soon calmed down, and I walked him back to his stables, trailing bits of wall and debris.

All that was left for us to do for that day was to make repairs and clear up!

Henry:
That was no horse, that was a fiery dragon....my horsey mother told me tales of dragon fights my horsey father had with a metal 'George' man on his back.

2. The hissing monster.....

Eddie:
In the early days of Henry's training we did a lot of long reining, walking several miles at a time, negotiating traffic and passing all kinds of obstacles. Our aim was to get Henry to respond to commands whilst desensitising him to vehicles, signs, bins, litter, road markings, other animals etc, in fact anything that was on or sharing the highways!

All was going very well and we were fairly happy and confident. Henry was building up trust and bonding with us really well. Then came the day of the lorry! One afternoon we were long reining along a well known route to the village. Henry was doing well responding to contact, verbal commands and allowing traffic to overtake.

We were all confident, infact so confident, Lorna was walking in front with Bazil on his lead. Exercise for all and everything was going really well..until...

Out of view and from around a sharp bend came the distinctive roar of a very, very big, hissing, spitting and venomous vehicle. Henry slid to a complete and rigid stop, ears back, heavy breathing, eyes wide(despite the blinkers).A typical 'time to run' pose! The huge monster soon appeared driving slowly towards us with hissing brakes, it's lights full on and hazards flashing!

This huge beast stopped and 'growled' just ten yards from us. There was only about six inches either side of it for us to go past. So we quickly, and stupidly, decided to pull into a small layby on our left hand side and let the monster pass, after all this was training.

We got to within touching distance of what we now saw was a commercial muck speader and just about the biggest HGV you can get! Henry decided enough was enough, and turned completely round in a second and I couldn't control him. Lorna was also helpless and unable get to Henry's head for control, because she was tangled up with Bazil, who was also trying to turn round and escape!

Another mistake on our part, because if Lorna didn't have to control the dog, she could have got to Henry's head to control and reassure him. As soon as Henry changed direction he was off like Red Rum, that famous racehorse! Hanging on tight to the reins, and connected to a terrified pony, I was soon belly surfing down the road at 30mph.I managed to hold on for a few seconds before Henry broke free and galloped off.

Luckily he was heading in the direction of his stable and his home. I was up in seconds and running after him, as was Lorna, dragging a terrified Bazil along behind her! We lost sight of Henry almost instantly as he charged off into the woods. It took us about 3 minutes to get to his stable yard...and there he was waiting at the gate, munching away at an old haynet as if nothing had happened!

Can you imagine our relief at finding our pony safe and home after this awful incident? How he had managed to get back, without becoming entangled in the trailing reins, is beyond us. Apart from a slight cut on his lip there was no damage. His tack of bridle, roller and reins were also in one piece. Lorna was distressed and out of breath but okay. So too was Bazil.

I got away fairly lightly with a black eye, split lip, cracked rib, cuts and bruises to my elbows and lower part of my body! Thank God I had listened to our LHHI and trainer, Chris, about safety..' always wear gloves when handling a horse'..I was wearing leather ones, and although they suffered some damage, and my knuckles shed some blood, I would have been much worse off without them!

Even though they are scuffed and ingrained with blood stains I still wear these gloves today for driving, as reminder of the incident and how much we learnt from it.

Henry:

I had started to trust my new owners, mum and dad, and tried to always do what they asked of me. But this snorting, steaming, hissing monster was something else. I can remember what my horsey mother told me when I was a very young and little foal, 'son..any sign of trouble run and ask questions later'...So I did.To tell the truth I really enjoyed my little run, even if dad did't!

3. The Vicar's wife....

Eddie:

In the early stages of our drives out together we could only go reasonable distances by passing through the village. Henry was gaining confidence and getting pretty good with traffic, cyclists and walkers. This was because the village, and in particular the pub, could get quite busy. On these drives out and back through the village we passed the vicarage twice, on our right going out, and our left coming back.

Then spring arrived, that time of year, when gardens need a lot of attention. Henry was quite happy on the way out, being use to this route now. Approaching the vicarage, with the fence on his right, he suddenly froze and his ears went back! Almost immediately a blond head popped up and from amoung the brambles, with snippers in hand, was the vicar's wife. 'Hello' she said.

It only took one more second for a terrified and snorting Henry to shoot off at a very rapid rate towards the pub. He really did, as the expression goes, fire on all four cylinders! On the way back the vicarage and fence were on his left. Up she popped again, with another 'Hello'. This was too much for an already nervous Henry. He was back home in a matter of seconds. I never knew a pony could move so fast!

The vicar's wife was always along that fence line, doing things that vicars' wives do, and Henry continued to be startled and scared at the same spot, journey out and journey back! For a month this continued to happen, despite our efforts to reassure him that this was infact a friend and not a troll. However, I will give the vicar's wife her due, despite continuing to pop up from behind the fence, she always had a kind word for our pony and sometimes even a nice carrot or handful of grass.

Eventually Henry got to grips with her and, after some time, we could stop and have a conversation whilst she comforted and stroked him. Which just goes to show 'God works in mysterious ways'

Henry:
I couldn't believe it, there I was just happily trotting through the village when I sensed an unknown and very dangerous creature skulking about in the brambles behind the fence to my right. It popped up, so I fled for my life to the pub. On the way back I thought it would be gone, but no, it popped up again but this time on my other side. I got Dad and Mum out of there and back home pretty sharpish.

Dad tried hard to reassure me that it was only a woman and also a friend, but she still kept jumping up, trying to spook me. Not just sometimes, every time, out and back. I hated that woman! However, a bit later, I got braver and didn't want to play her silly games anymore. After all what kind of human likes scaring small ponies! Eventually, we sort of became friends and she use to stroke me and give me treats. She still scares me sometimes though!

4. The Pheasant....

Eddie:
Henry was progressing reasonably well on the road, so we decided to have a little relax and take him alongside woodland on private land(with permission).What could be nicer and safer? No hard road, no traffic, no cyclists. 'Just us three enjoying life in perfect harmony of mind, body and spirit'. I guess the grass was about four inches

high and Henry was into a lovely trot along the track. Head up, ears up, alert and happy, happy happy.

Suddenly, with a loud squawk and flapping of wings, an adult pheasant literally exploded between Henry's legs before beating a noisy and hasty departure into the air. For a split second Henry halted and froze..he shook from head to hoof..then in the next second, a microsecond, he fired both barrels(back hooves)into the dashboard of our carriage, then reversed like lightning, pushing the carriage and us into the undergrowth!

He continued to reverse(something we didn't know he could do)closer and closer to a large oak tree. I yelled, and Lorna was off the carriage in a trice to get to Henry's head for control. Henry gave another very hard kick to the dashboard, followed by a 'rear up' that was so high I nearly fell off the carriage, then a bolt forwards at full throttle!

Lorna managed somehow to grab hold of his underhalter, I pulled back on the reins, and together we quickly halted him. Thank God for following the rule of never going out without an underhalter and capable groom. Without Lorna it would have been a catastrophe! We managed to get home in one piece..and again, in our limited driving experience...shaken but not stirred.

Lorna:

I remember that incident with absolute clarity. The urgency in Eddie's voice to get to Henry's head for control. It was, in all honesty, no mean feat. I was so thankful that I had spent many hours at Henry's head,standing and reassuring him, leading and walking in front of him, gaining his trust in me as a safe place. I can still see his terrified face, ears back, wide eyes and snorting breath.

It took a full minute or two for him to focus on me and calm down. We did actually remount the carriage and drive him home, I suppose to prove to us all that it was nothing we couldn't handle together, but that incident was scary!

Henry:

I can't remember much except I had nearly been got by a horrible monster that tried to rip my chest and eat me. I was so scared that all I could do was raise up my front hooves and kick out with the back ones. But suddenly mum was there to save me and I could hear dad's voice from the carriage behind me, chasing the winged monster away.

5. The Squirrel....

Lorna:

We had decided on a four wheeler ten mile long drive, it was a new route and in places took us through lovely avenues of trees, in some places with overhanging and interlocking branches. Eddie was as usual, happy in his comfort zone, driving from the front right seat. I was also very secure and happy on my back step position, glancing at the map and always on the lookout for hazards.

Henry was in a lovely determined trot, when suddenly a grey, furry creature fell directly in front of us from the canopy of trees above us. It squealed as Henry went over it, then it raced away with a wild backward glance. Surprise, Surprise, Henry didn't even notice and kept on going, in his determined trot, as if nothing had happened!

Eddie and I had a hysterical laughing fit, and a car coming towards us steered well clear of these two lunatic maniacs on a horse drawn carriage.

Henry:

What squirrel???

6. The Red Kite....

Eddie:

We had almost made it home on the four wheeler. It had been a lovely drive and Henry had dropped to a walk to cool down. Suddenly out of a large tree a kite (Bird of Prey) swept down with talons barred, only changing its course, inches away from Henry's blinkers, at the very last second! Henry took it all in his stride. But it could have been a real disaster for us all if Henry had spooked and bolted.

Believe it or not this happened several more times at the same spot. What all this was about we shall never really know, but it was eventually sorted out with help from my whip...contact was made...and the kite was never seen again. Just another thing for us to think about!

Henry:
I hated that bird and was so glad dad got it with his whip!

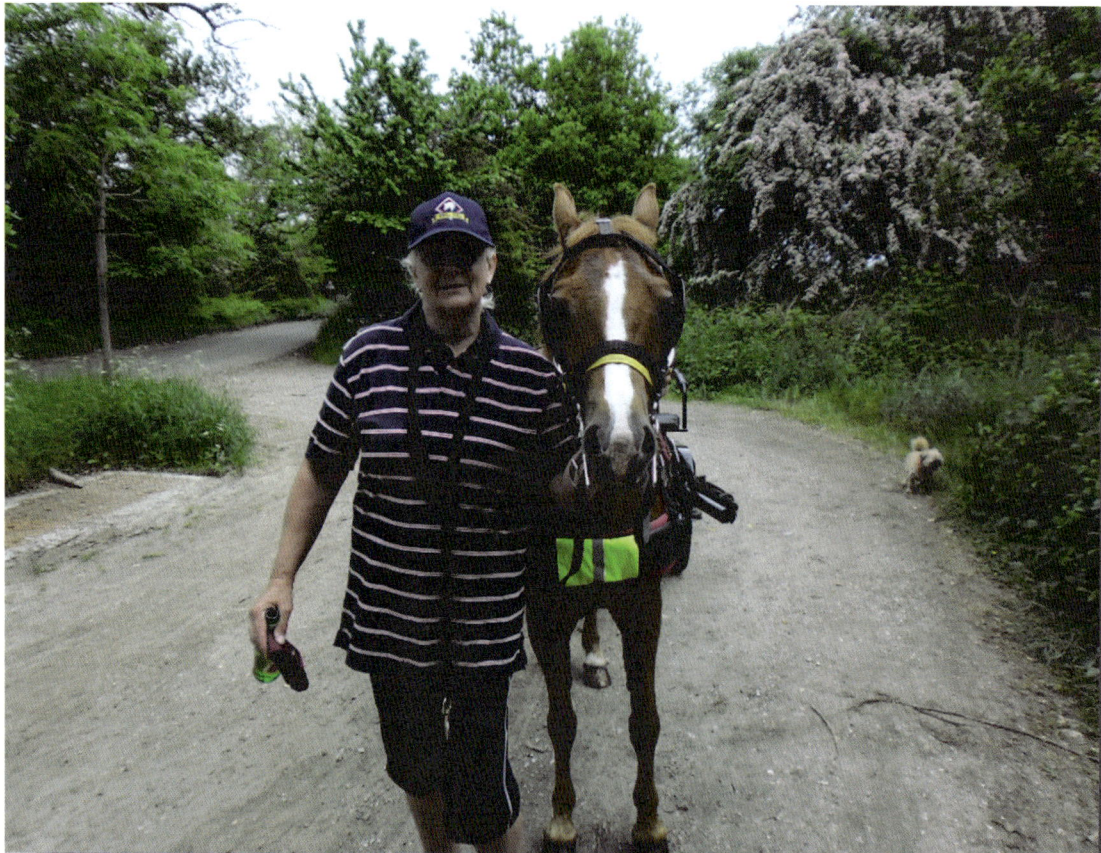

Lorna taking control at Henry's head

Chapter Ten...

Stories to tell of Trips and Slips

1. The Mounting Block...

Lorna:

As part of Henry's training and confidence building we thought it would be a good idea to get him standing at a mounting block. We tried to do this several times with limited success. Eddie would stand at the top of the mounting block, but hard as I tried, I could not get Henry to stand alongside it. He just twisted and turned this way and that! Anything but stand steady next to the block.

One day, Eddie was standing on the top of the block and I finally managed to get Henry alongside it. Like a martial artist Eddie lifted his leg and rested his heel on Henry's back, what an achievement! However, at this particular moment, when all was going well, I lost concentration. Henry decided enough was enough, he 'walked on' instead of 'standing still' and tripped me up with his front hooves.

There I was flat on my back, with a pony walking all over me in an attempt to get to his stable and fast. Eddie was helpless, at the top the mounting block, so couldn't get to Henry's head for control. It's fair to say I was walked all over by a pony with shiny shoes! I had a couple of bruises, minor cuts and a black eye.

It could have been a lot worse and a lesson to me to never lose concentration with Henry, or any other horse again!

Henry:
Sorry Mum!

2. Rocket Girl....

Eddie:
It was on one of the rare occasions that we had a visit from Lorna's daughter Sandra. Sandra, who apart from being delighted to see her Mum, was very keen to meet Henry for the first time. Just so you understand, I say rare occasions because whenever Sandra visits, I can't resist the temptation to 'Tease and wind her up'. However she always gives as good as she gets...but not on this occasion!

So this very beautiful, young and twenty something lady, found herself walking to the stables with her wicked stepfather to meet Henry! Whilst mother stayed behind to cook dinner, Sandra was being introduced to Henry. The introduction went fine, butter wouldn't melt in Henry's mouth, as he was stroked and fed titbits. I'd swear, that he looked at me, and then at the huge stable clock, with the devil in his eyes!

It was supper time..and I just couldn't resist it. It was only about 50 yards to get to his stable and supper from where he was tied up. I knew from experience that Henry could travel this distance in seconds with me in hot pusuit, faster than Usain Bolt, through the yard, to the most important thing in his life...supper!

As Henry continued to look doe eyed at Sandra, I innocently, asked her if she would like to walk Henry to his supper. She enthusiastically agreed. She held the untied lead rope and asked Henry to 'walk on' he obeyed and did so very positively. In fact he did a very fast trot, with this young lady in an almost horizontal position, hanging on for dear life behind him. She actually looked like a very fast rocket.

Nearer the stable his trot became a gallop and still with Sandra in tow! At his stable he suddenly stopped, turned sharp left into his stall and supper! Sandra was ejected into the corner of the stable but still managed to smile as she dusted herself down and stood up. I couldn't help a secret snigger...got her again!

Henry:
That was fun!!!

Sandra:
Never again!

Lorna:
Naughty boys!!

3. The Ditch....

Eddie:
This incident happened in the early days of our driving experience. We were on the two wheeler, thank God, enjoying a lovely plod to a small, far away village. I was now occasionally handing the reins and control to Lorna so she could enjoy driving such a lovely creature, and in the event of disaster, be able to drive home with confidence. Conditions were perfect, no wind, not raining, but slightly wet.

Lorna was happily driving and Henry was being quite well behaved, that is until he spied two puddles, yes puddles, out of the corner of his eye. In an instant, he shied big time and changed direction by ninety degrees, dragging us and the carriage into a huge ditch hidden by a large clump of nettles at the side of the road! I wasn't quite quick enough to take the reins and control.

Poor Lorna just had to hold on for her life. Henry had now been steered into the ditch and was up to his shoulders in nettles and muddy slime. It only took us seconds to get to Henry's head and take control, reversing him out onto the road and safety. By that time we were all cursing the nettles and the stinking water. Back on the road we headed home for a shower...including Henry and the carriage!

That night we laughed until we cried!

Lorna:

It took a long time before I would agree to take the reins again. I have learnt from that incident that anything can happen, at any time, and in a split second in carriage driving. Now two years on I quite often confidently and safely drive Henry.

Henry:

Mum and Dad never believed me, but I swear there were two monsters in those puddles..just one more step and they would have gobbled us all up. They still remind me of that day, whenever they see any puddles, just to wind me up!

4. Wheels on Fire........

Eddie:

Lorna and I had decidced to go for a short drive on the two wheeler, which was fitted with very useful disc brakes .Before it got too dark we set off down the lane. Henry was soon into a trot, he seemed to be managing but struggling a bit. His nostrils were flared and his breathing a bit heavier than normal. He just seemed to be working harder than usual but we couldn't work out what the problem was.

Strangely, there seemed to be a burning smell in the air that was following us down the road. Then we realised as the wheels started to shudder that the disc brakes may have locked and siezed. We 'whoad' Henry, who turned his head round to look at us with great relief. Lorna went to Henry's head(for control,as usual)whilst I hopped off to examine the wheels and saw smoke wafting from the discs.

Then I did something really stupid, with my bare hand I grabbed the disc to see if it was hot! It was so hot it welded my naked hand flesh to the hard steel!!

Lorna:

Whilst I held Henry's head, Eddie crawled under the cart to see what the problem was, then I heard a loud scream followed by swear words of the highest rating. Eddie was jumping around and blowing mightily on his red inflamed hand. Luckily we were not far from home and managed, by walking and pushing, to get Henry and the cart back to the stable yard. This incident just goes to show how strong Henry's inner strenght was.

With sheer courage and determination he had pulled that cart along, doing what was expected of him despite the odds. What other pony would do that for his masters? Our pony had guts!

Henry:

That was hard work..really hard work. But I dug in deep and did it for mum and dad.. and always will.

5. Reach for the sky....

Eddie:

On this particular afternoon we took Henry out on the 2 wheel exercise cart into the countryside. We decided to patronise a hostlery we rarely used. In the car parking area Lorna was standing with Henry, whilst he was nibbling the grass verge and.. sneaking bits of hedge into his mouth. I was chatting happily, over a small glass of beverage, to the publican. Suddenly, storm clouds appeared overhead and the thought of a soaking appealed to none of us! We quickly took to our seated positions on the cart and proceeded to the exit, where we halted to check for any oncoming traffic. Henry appeared a little reluctant to 'whoa' to my verbal command, so I gave a little pressure on the reins as was usual in times like this. Henry promptly did something he had never done before. In a second he reared up on his hind legs. His body was vertical to the cart, tipping it backwards and with us in it! In fact it felt as if our heads were going to make contact with the ground behind us. In a thrice Henry came back down again, onto all fours and stood still, but he was obviously not happy about something. The occupants of an oncoming white van witnessed the whole spectacle. Both the rather scruffy looking driver and passenger gave us huge smiles and a thumbs up before driving off with much waving. They obviously thought we had made Henry rear on purpose for their entertainment!

Lorna:

At Eddie's rapid command I was off the cart (for nearly a second time!)I went straight to Henry's head, he was standing still, but in some distress. After a couple of seconds of looking at him I could see what the cause of the problem was. He had something small poking out of his mouth, it was trapped by the metal mouth bit and sticking into his tongue. Carefully I prised his jaw open and removed the offending item...a twig from the hedge had snapped into his mouth whilst he was munching at the pub. This had caused him pain when Eddie had applied contact on the reins. The sudden pain had caused Henry to rear up. The piece of hedge removed, we were soon on our way...all well again despite receiving a good soaking for our troubles..To see your horse rearing up in front of you is both a scary and amazing sight to see. Luckily we came to no harm!

Henry:

I tried my best for dad, but had to let him know my mouth was hurting. I had felt good up till then though so will never touch a hedge again.

48

Chapter Eleven...

Only another six months

Lorna:

As our continuing training progressed on and on, Eddie's answer to any question, problem or hiccup would be 'Only another six months and he will be a perfect driving pony'. That six months forecast was multiplied by four, and it was only then that Eddie stopped saying that famous phase 'In six months'. In just under two years we had tried many combinations of carriages ,tack, training aids and techniques and at last we considered we had got it about right. Neither we or Henry are perfect or foolproof. But we are happy, enjoying our time together, always learning and looking to the next six months! A team...Team Henry.

The Team Henry motto.....

Henry:

Bolt first...run fast...ask questions later!

Eddie:

Only trust a horse as far as you can throw it!

lorna:

Expect the unexpected and stay sharp!

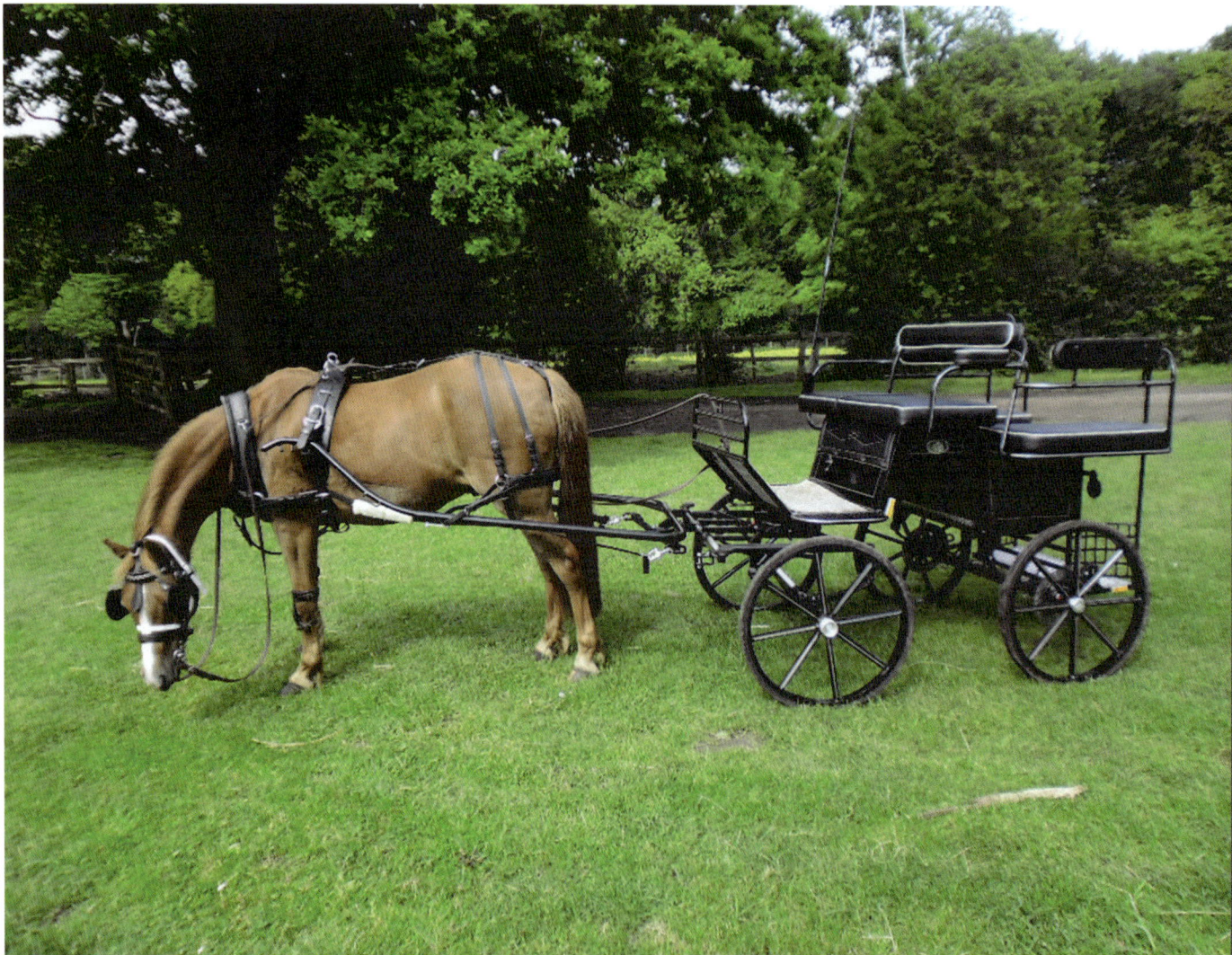

Henry and the 4 wheeler

Chapter Twelve..

Looking forwards to another six months!

Eddie:

The three of us continued to work together and have further adventures. Henry had dark days when the pain returned to his feet, so he didn't do so much driving. We had a plan for a new life fo him, maybe in the showring, showing in hand...just showing off really!

Believe it or not, if treated with respect, he would now take a light person on his back. So the icing on the cake would be when a young rider, could put a saddle on his back, and ride him in the training arena on sand that doesn't hurt his feet. He would have some new adventures and we would shed some tears in pride.

You would have to look very hard to find a kinder, more well mannered pony than Henry. He still tried and managed, without being caught out, to be naughty and cheeky. With the return of laminitis we knew we would have fewer driving experiences with him, but he would be with us for the remainder of his days.

To finish on a good note ,God gave us a gift in the form of a rescue cob, Charlie.A bay coloured monster of a horse(in comparison to Henry!)Charlie had been loaned to us by his rescuers, very lovely people, who thought we could give him a better life as a driving horse.

To cut another long story short, it has taken us 'six months' in total to change a frightened, unsure and 'untidy' horse into a beautiful, responsive, loving, driving and riding animal. Again, a few genuine friends have helped us out with his problems. But it is actually Henry who has taught us all we know and made the transition so easy.

They both shared the same field and yard, becoming pretty good mates, and at times, very affectionate towards each other. Charlie, at first, used his weight and muscle to push Henry around a bit, but believe me Henry is the brainy one! He got Charlie into so much by trouble by leading the way and always managing not to get caught out himself! Henry has taught Charlie many things....To undo a variety of knots and free himself from a wall! To not only stand on our feet, but also to twist the hoof around to maximise the pain! To nip your bottom when your back is turned! To tip everything out of the grooming bucket and chew it! To rope chew! To frisk your pocket for titbits! To change direction when driving, as soon as the masters loose their concentration!

These are just a few of the tricks Henry has passed on to Charlie. However, we sometimes wonder if Henry has also taught Charlie, in spite of Charlie's cruel past, to trust and love us and do his best for us. We love them both. So thank you Henry for everthing you have taught us too!

Chapter Thirteen...

The Dream.As told by Henry.

I really have had enough now and I am fed up with this pain in my feet. The pain is nearly always there, it is sometimes so bad that I have to lie down. Sometimes I have to hobble like a very old horse. I am not fit anymore, I don't look as good as I use to and can no longer work. I feel useless even though Mum and Dad, who love me to bits, do everything they can to make me comfortable and keep me clean.

I have had enough of vets, needles, medicines, bland tasting food and bandages. But worst of all they have taken my work shoes off! I can only graze on sweet grass for a little while, and my hay tastes wet and horrible. I can't exercise either, because it hurts my feet. I hate staying in my room for days on end and, because I can't get out, I am miserable.

But I do have hope and a dream that one night I will go to sleep, a nice long, lovely sleep and wake up completely cured, just like that! I will once again be a normal pony! Trotting through the village and up the hill.I will work like I used to with the sweat steaming of my body. All the people that see me will admire me and Mum and Dad will be so proud to be showing me off. Fit and happy again!

I will be so happy and proud because, I am once again, putting on my best black and gold harness that shines in the sun. I will get into my wheels again and trot faster than I ever did, I will turn better than I ever did and stand still when my master tells me..... This is my Dream!

Henry harnessed up and ready for a drive

Chapter Fourteen...

Good bye my friend

Eddie:

Henry's bout of laminitis, with sore feet, continued through his time with us. Laterly, he also developed another life threatening, secondary condition to laminitis, EMS(Equinine Metabolic Syndrome)Now we needed to restrict his food and grazing further, also he had to take maxium doses of prescribed medication to slow down the inevitable disease progression. It became obvious the road work was also taking its toll on his hooves, despite regular farriering, special shock padding, and shoes. The trouble was he was so fit and strong now, that it was of no benefit to him to reduce his mileage. Although we did cut back on the road miles, we could sense that in spite of his illness, he was not happy with this.

We are sure he enjoyed his adventures, hours and hard work out on the road with us. Trying to control his condition, keeping him fit and happy, proved to be an almost impossible task. We extensively researched the condition of laminitis and it was with a heavy heart we learnt, that not only are laminitic ponies prone to EMS, but that 75% of laminitic ponies die from the condition. After Henry's last drive, on grass believe it or not, he developed an abscess to his right fore.

The vet was called, he prescribed poultice treatments, antibiotics and maximum drugs for the pain. Henry was put on box rest for about three weeks. The box rest, twice daily poulticing , bandaging and medication to fight the infection made Henry very unhappy. As a side effect to treatment he also developed diarrhoea. So he also had the indignity of being washed frequently.

His spirit seemed to go down daily, in spite of much love, attention and grooming from us. We would often sneak up quietly and secretly, peer over the stable door to see him lying dejected on the floor. On these occasions he would always struggle to his feet to greet us. As the days went on his condition got worse, and his spirit got weaker. In the final day of his life he could not even take two steps. I had known for a while what decision was awaiting me.

With a grim and defeated heart I called the vet back in. After a quick examination the vet told us it was a hopeless case. The humane thing to do would be to put Henry to sleep immediately. After a shot of strong pain killers we managed to slowly walk Henry a short distance across the yard, to a peaceful and private grassy place, where he was finally and gracefully put to sleep, gently collapsing to his knees and then down.

Within a second the spark of life left Henry and we said a final goodbye and thank you, with tears rolling like waterfalls down our cheeks. Although we were prepared for this, we were absolutely devastated and in shock. Peter, our vet comforted us by telling us we had done everything possible for Henry, but this really was an impossible situation. However, the nagging doubts and uncertainty will always haunt me.

Did we do enough or too little to treat this condition .I shall never know. But what I do know is that Henry would not have liked being stabled for hours at a time, and only let out for very short times on a barren piece of pasture. That is not the natural life nature intended for a pony. We had lost our brave, beautiful and hard working pony. A really, really special friend and part of our family. Wherever he is now we hope the grass is always green, the sun is shining and he is running and kicking up his hooves. Free from pain at last.

It personally took me many weeks to be able to cope with this loss it was the most miserable and sadest time for me. As always, Lorna was the strong one, so with her help, I started to get a grip on myself. Our recent addition, Charlie the cob, was very demanding at the time, so training and driving him seemed to ease my sorrow.

We like to think that somehow a part of Henry is with us in Charlie. Thank you Charlie for pulling us through. You, like Henry, have a huge heart.

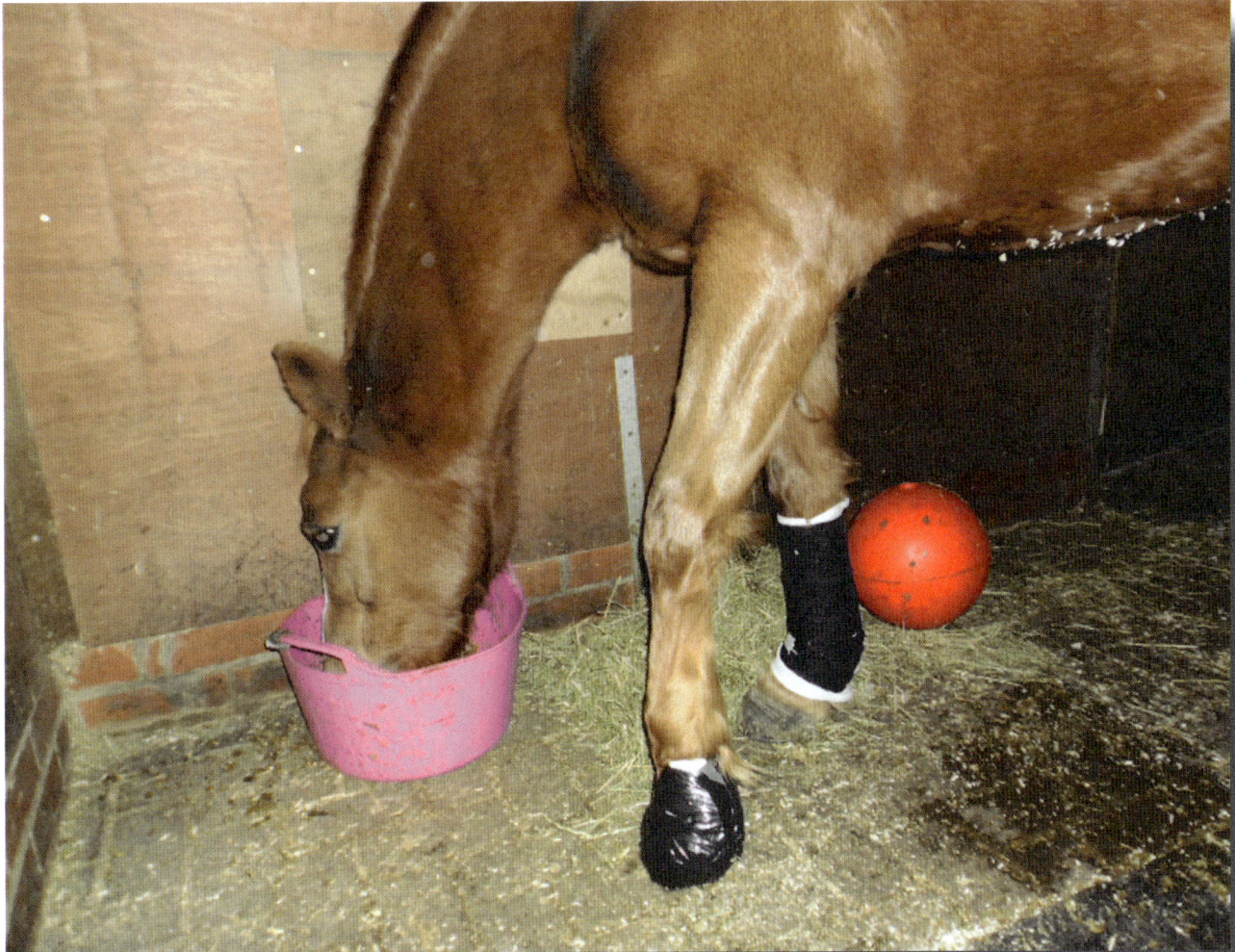

Henry with a foot abscess

Charlie and Eddie out for a drive

A final word...

After reading our story about our journey with Henry, I imagine there are a few questions you might like to ask.

Was it all worth it?

It was absolutely worth it. Yes, we spent a lot of money we didn't need to. We spent a lot of time we didn't need to. We put ourselves in danger many times. What was the result? A pony we trained ourselves, to eventually go out carriage driving together on the road, giving us endless pleasure and fun. We made him what he was and he was totally our pony. We actually turned a nervous wreck of a pony into a forward going, brave and well mannered boy!

Would we do it all again?

Yes, and we have done so with several other horses and ponies. To be honest they have all been easier, simply because we learnt all our triumphs and mistakes as a team with Henry.

That beautiful boy taught us so much and we are forever indebited to him. Whenever we look at our many photographs of him we are filled with pride. However we wouldn't recommend anyone as green as we were to take on such a difficult task. Our advice would be to first seek proffessional help and guidance. You may not have nearly as much fun as we did but you will be much safer! However, if you do follow our way, in the end you will have your own carriage driving pony, trained by you to your needs, standard and expectation. So make your own conclusion from this final word. Although Henry is no longer physically with us, we are now well into our fourth year of carriage driving. We now drive our lovely cob Charlie, but that is another story yet to be told, just as hair raising and as much fun as it always used to be....We love it and do so in memory of Henry.

Fact File:

Foaled... 20 April 2002

Chestnut gelding, Welsh pony section B

Height 13 hands

Purchased by us-10/06/2011

Drove... approx 1,700 miles between the counties of Bucks and Oxon

RIP...29 November 2013...Free from laminitis and to roam and graze at last.

Acknowledgements:

With our heartfelt thanks to Chris, April, Glenn and Dean for their friendship, support and advice.

Henry

Printed in Great Britain
by Amazon